VISUAL CONTENT

120 User-Friendly Free Tools to Create an Awesome Visual Content for Your Blog and Social Media Even You Are Not Good at Designing

Sage T

Contents

Introduction

I want to thank you and congratulate you for purchasing the book, *"Visual Content"- 120 User-Friendly Free Tools to Create an Awesome Visual Content for Your Blog and Social Media Even You Are Not Good at Designing.*

Visual content is very much essential for a marketer. Be it advertising, or social media post, and it's been proven that visual content is a lot more useful than plain text. Hence, we need to be creative and develop better visual content every day. Being a marketer, time is the essence. You cannot spend hours on developing a pure visual content, neither could you depend on your design staff to work on your idea and give you immediate result.

If you are right in Photoshop yourself and dedicate time on it, then that's a different story. But if you think Photoshop is tricky and tedious

or you don't have enough time to experiment on
it. Then this Book is for you

v

so. The presentation of the information is without contract or any type of guarantee assurance.

The publisher and author of this book have made every effort to prepare a book that provides top results to the readers. However, the publisher and author make no warranties about the applicability, or the completeness regarding its content. The information contained here is strictly for educational purposes only. So, if you decide to apply the strategies or ideas discussed in this book, you will be taking full responsibilities for your actions. There cannot be any guarantees that you will earn money applying the strategies or ideas discussed here.

The trademarks that are used are without any consent, and the publication of the trademark is without permission or backing by the trademark owner. All trademarks and brands within this book are for clarifying purposes only and are the owned by the owners themselves, not affiliated with this document.

Section 1: Free Photo Databases

Tool 1: Wikimedia Commons is one of the most commonly utilized and the largest online image databases. Its content is known to be majorly free of copyrights, with some still being under some legal restrictions. The website itself does provide elaboration on how to utilize its content and how to manage when the needed image happens to be copyright restricted or at least unguaranteed to be copyright free.

Tool 2: Pixabay is an online image platform, the content of which is established by photographers around the world who contribute with their pictured work that is, in turn, is characterized by high quality and freedom of copyright restrictions. You are enabled via this website to search for the images of your preference with the aid of filtration options, with which you can browse for what you want by some criteria such as the photographer, type of the used camera, category and color.

Tool 3: Unsplash is another online community established by photographers around the world who are inclined away from traditional photography and imagery. These photographers do via this website provide you with hundreds of thousands of various pictures that are accessible to you without copyright restrictions or the need to request permission for taking any further procedure such as modification and distribution.

Tool 4: Flickr Commons is another image database that provides you access to plenty of images contributed from not only the United States but also numerous other regions of our planet. It is known to be supported by worldwide archives and libraries databases. It is also declared that the likeliness of stumbling across an image unguaranteed to be copyright free is still present although mild, which in turn entails repeated checking before deciding on seizing the chosen image for the intended personal purposes.

Tool 5: <u>Public Domain Pictures</u> is a website that harbors plenty of public domain images characterized by being free and of high quality. Nevertheless, it is not considered much of a preferred choice for so many, and this is attributed to some disadvantages that comprise the following:

-The website includes the premium membership option, with which you would be granted full access to all the available content. This simply means you would most probably enjoy restricted mobility on that database, especially if you encounter an image that entails a premium subscription, so as for you to be able to seize it.

-It is important to do a careful check on each chosen image for the license. This is because you would be subject to find yourself having to credit the author or the original uploader or owner of the image, an event that is in turn not really favorable for commercial designs.

-You would find yourself quite often in need to ensure obtaining a release of some image categories, especially those including people, houses, and properties.

Tool 6: <u>Magdeleine</u> is a free stock photography website that more or less does not resemble stock. It requires selectivity and attention while searching for images of preference as some of the content still entails attribution. Through this database, you can navigate through images by searching by some criteria such as the colors and categories.

Tool 7: <u>Old Book Illustrations</u> is a database with a Victorian atmosphere, on which you can get access to plenty of relevant illustrations taken from old books and reflective pictures. This database can be considered a good choice if you wish to include some vintage vibes on your space to be created.

Tool 8: <u>Public Domain Vectors</u> includes an enormity of public domain vectors that are all licensed under the CCo (no copyright preserved) label. You can obtain what you want from that database via downloading them as SVG, EPS and AI files.

Tool 9: <u>1 Million Free Pictures</u> is another image database which is described as such simply because all its content belongs to one author who is themselves the founder of the website. You can search for the images of your preference using the galleries built within the platform. It is noteworthy to notify about being cautious when using images that include people, artwork, trademarks and properties, as it is believed in no releases being obtained for these images.

Tool 10: <u>ISO Republic</u> provides more than 500 images free for personal and commercial utilization, without any need for attributions or requesting permission. The built-in gallery is consistently expanding in its content.

Tool 11: <u>Free Stock Photos</u> harbors a collection of stock images and clip art, being classified as both copyright free and reserved. This hence entails your attention while in the search and selecting process.

Tool 12: <u>Realistic Shots</u> does entirely include images under the CCo license, characterized – as so many states – by looking like anything but being stock images. This database consistently adds seven new images on a weekly basis.

Tool 13: <u>Startup Stock Photos</u> harbors CCo labeled images that mainly revolve around comfortable working environments, technologies and general creativity.

Tool 14: <u>Jay Mantri</u> is a database named after its establisher who is a professional photographer. It includes plenty of uploads that represent Jay's work and comprise sceneries from around the world. The

6

entire content requires no attributions or permission requests as it is categorized as CCo.

Tool 15: <u>The British Library</u> is another good choice for those engaged in Vintage style. This database embraces a massive collection of scanned 17th, 18th and 19th-century books pages, with their inclusions ranging from typography, to instruments and animals and to other remarkable elements.

Tool 16: <u>Public Domain Archive</u> compiles a collection of high-quality images that belong to both vintage and contemporary categories.

Tool 17: <u>Viintage</u> embraces a massive collection of relevant presentations that mainly include posters and advertisements, which are in turn highly likely to undergo renovation.

Tool 18: <u>The Public Domain Review</u> was established in 2011 to attract audiences inclined to obtain more material related to history, including illustrations, images, texts, audio and films.

Tool 19: DesignerPics.com has been founded by an Indian designer based on his experience which was characterized by ultimate difficulty in finding appropriate quality-free images. The database hosts his own work that can be utilized without the need for attribution or permission.

Tool 20: StockSnap is another image database on which the entire content is labeled as CC0 with no need for attributions or permissions. You are enabled via this website to view images by their date of upload, the number of views and their popularity level.

Tool 21: Pexels includes high-quality license-free images, many of which are gathered from other free image websites. The content expands at a minimum rate of 70 images added on a weekly basis.

Tool 22: Death To The Stock Photo is another website that regularly outsources to you image packs for free download. The option of premium subscription is present in case you are interested in providing some support to the photographers who have found that website. This can be fulfilled by purchasing a monthly subscription of 15 dollars.

Tool 23: Snapwire Snaps expands its collection on a weekly basis at a rate of seven images. The entire collection is labeled as CC0. This platform was basically established to connect professional photographers around the world with professional companies that are in need of custom photography, and afterward included the previously mentioned link for the sake of the audience who wish to make benefit of license-free photos.

Tool 24: EveryStockPhoto is a specialized search engine in the field of free stock images. It enables you to gain access to stock images present on other prominent free stock image domains such as Wikimedia, Flickr and also NASA. As the spectrum of search is quite broad, it is highly recommended to check carefully for the presence or absence of

9

licensing restriction in the items appealing to you to make use of.

Tool 25: Negative Space is a contemporary database hosting high-resolution images revolving mainly around categories and forms of "spaces" such as workspaces, open spaces and so forth. You can do filter your search results by this criterion as well as with category and colors of target images.

Tool 26: Foodies Feed is an excellent option to seek in case you are constructing an online platform for a restaurant. It hosts plenty of good food images that do not resemble those prevalent fake ones and that are undoubtedly available for use without a need for attributions.

Tool 27: Fancy Crave has been founded by the professional photographer "Igor Ovsyannikov" who has curated plenty of high-quality, high-resolution and license-free images on it. The collection of image exponentially grows at a rate of two images daily.

Tool 28: <u>SpaceX</u> is a domain within Flickr that provides you access to plenty of pictures taken outside the Earth, with all being available to utilize freely.

Tool 29: <u>Barn Images</u> was created by two Latvian professional photographers with the aim of breaking the tradition of stock images, having described their database as non-stock. The collection is consistently growing on a daily basis, and the entire content is available for commercial use, although it is recommended to read what they have narrated on their website regarding the license.

Tool 30: <u>The Pic Pac</u> is a database of a different type as it follows the principle of "Pay what you want". In other words, the content is basically not necessarily free and requires purchasing. The visitor is allowed the chance to pay the price they prefer so as for them to purchase the image of their preference, and to be able to make use of it. New photo packs are added regularly on Mondays for purchase. All the content as labeled as CCo.

Section 2: Free Photo Editing Tools

It is well known that not everyone is capable of utilizing Adobe Photoshop and other resembling photo editing programmes for reasons related to pricing, the complexity of utilization and difficulty to learn, and sometimes all of these.

Photo editing can be as simple as cropping an image to be as complex as altering its main features and manipulating its contents. The internet could also ease the obstacle of photo editing programmes via providing some available online specialized platforms, be they payable of free. Some of the free ones chosen to you are as follows:

Tool 31: Pixlr is considered one of the first line tools for free online photo editing, with plenty of photo editing tools being supported and available to utilize. Pixlr allows you to take control of multiple effects regarding color, cropping, resizing

13

and other parameters. You can seek either the Editor or the Express versions, depending on the level of editing you prefer to apply. Moreover, the edited picture can be saved both on your computer and on the platform online.

Tool 32: iPiccy is another photo editing base with a multiplicity of editing tools that allows you to moderate several parameters and elements of the photo being worked on. Saving options are available, with the possibility of saving your picture after editing on your computer and sharing – as per your preference – on social media, including Facebook.

Tool 33: FotoFlexer is considered one of the marvelous editing platforms, for it includes plenty of special features that are fun to use and work with. Some of these features include manipulating even the slightest details such as the red-eye remover, pinching and bulging effects and editing borders. You are also allowed to apply effects on a particular area of the image, instead of the entirety of it. You can import images for editing from not only your computer but also other online image databases and through URL pasting.

Tool 34: Adobe Photoshop Express Editor is the free version of Adobe's photo editor that is available online for public use by non-designers. Despite hosting a limited number and basic features out of those present in the advanced Photoshop versions, it is still considered approachable and flexible to use, with the availability of red-eye removal, alteration of color saturation, white balancing and other tools being accessible.

Tool 35: Fotor is another cool interface for online editing with which you can apply particular changes to your pictures through brief clicks. Basic tools such as cropping and adjusting the color intensity of the image are available.

Tool 36: Picozu is characterized by allowing multiple tabs at once, which means you can work on multiple images simultaneously. It also supports the auto-saving peculiarity, which is certainly helpful in protecting your work from being abruptly lost for any reason. Some advanced features such as adjustment of layers and multiple filters are present to make use of.

Tool 37: PhotoCat is an online editor that is believed to be more or less compatible with the standards of so many photo editing enthusiasts as it hosts some attractive and essential features. These features include the basic typical ones of cropping and adding frames, plus the spray effect, blemish remover and many more.

Tool 38: piZap despite having a small interface, is still considered a good tools for having some good features. Some of these features include overlaying multiple images and adding glittered texts. There is also a special feature that allows creating your own stickers from images.

Tool 39: <u>Cut My Pic!</u> Is quite easy and smooth to use. All that you are requested to do is to upload the image of your preference, select the effects that you find appropriate and which are provided by this base. You can preview the edited image before proceeding further. You are also allowed the chance to save the edited image either on your computer or on social media.

Tool 40: <u>Quick Picture Tools</u> from its name, we may state that it implies its functionality on a narrower spectrum, with only about ten editing tools being provided for utilization.

Section 3: Free Cover Creator

Tool 41: Canva Book Cover Maker is one of the most flexible and prevalent free cover creators, being appealed to by plenty of non-designers who wish to go for the self-publication journey. This platform allows you the opportunity to utilize either your own imagery or that present on the base to design and construct your cover. Its flexibility is attributed to enabling you to take control of every single part of the cover, making the designing process almost completely under your moderation.

Tool 42: Cover Creator is an online cover creator integrated with Amazon's CreateSpace, which is a platform for self-publishing. This means you can gain access to both bases as you create an account on CreateSpace

Tool 43: Adobe Spark is a facility provided by Adobe which can be seized by non-designers at their very beginnings in the course of cover creation. This tool is available for free only temporarily.

Tool 44: <u>Poster My Wall</u> is a more or less good choice for a non-designer who wishes to comprehend, at least in an introductory way, how book covers are being designed. It is however limited regarding the quantity of available covers, which renders the spectrum of choice quite restricted.

Tool 45: <u>BookWright</u> is a branch of Blurb, allowing you to create an attractive cover for your book. You are also allowed the chances of:

-Downloading the programme and working offline with it.
-Insert page numbers to your book pages.
-Assign a unique free ISBN

19

Section 4: Free Logo Creating Tools

Tool 46: <u>Canva</u> is known as the leading online logo creating tool, offering templates that are both paid and free. You may initially start with one of the templates available on its platform and do the alterations you desire, and in case you are not pleased enough, you may work with other external options or with the aid of the elements available in the Canva library. A disadvantage of this platform is that the templates available are accessible by everyone, which increases the likeliness of stumbling across a logo that to some extent resemble yours. This should not be worried about that much as creativity can be of great help at such times.

Tool 47: <u>Free Logo Services</u> is another logo creator that allows downsizing the variants displayed to you by the style you wish to go for, which makes the process of work more convenient and time-saving.

You can also via this website create custom business cards with your created logo on them.

Tool 48: <u>Free Logo Design</u> is a tool you can use by simply typing the name of your company, previewing plenty of available templates, applying the necessary adjustments and afterward downloading the finalized design for free. Be attentive that you shall pay 59$ if you wish to download your logo with better quality and a higher resolution.

Tool 49: <u>Graphic Springs</u> does to some extent resembles the preceding tool regarding the process of work. Nevertheless, it is noteworthy to highlight that the entire creating process is free whereas the download needs 20$ to be fulfilled.

Tool 50: <u>LogoMakr</u> offers you a flexibly used programme that allows you to search firstly for the appropriate shapes and icons, editing their appearance, writing the needed word or text and customizing it. Downloading the logo is free but with some restrictions that may be inconvenient to many users such as receiving a low-quality logo and having the platform retaining the credit.

Tool 51: <u>UCraft</u> is generally a website builder that offers not only logo creating but also web templates, free cloud hosting, and even more. It harbors over 200,000 icons you can explore and use in your process. Downloading your work is free of charge.

Tool 52: <u>Online Logo Maker</u> is smooth to start logo design with, with a lot of templates and fonts available. You are free to choose from their already designed symbols or from your own image collection. A free registration allows saving the work for future reference, and paid subscription allows a chance of downloading a higher resolution logo.

Tool 53: <u>Designmantic</u> can be used by choosing the preferred style, entering the name, selecting the appropriate industry category, customizing the logo of choice and downloading it after accomplishing work. The latter, however, always entails a monetary fee. This base after all does not provide limitedly free work, which means those who do not pay to download would be basically doing not more than learning and enjoying what the tool has to provide but without significant utilization in further steps.

Tool 54: <u>Shopify</u> provides to you overall the tools required to establish your own online store, including of course a tool for creating an appropriate and appealing logo

Tool 55: <u>Logo Type Maker</u> with over 200 fonts, over 1,000 professional templates, and over 600,000 vector shapes, you can unleash your creativity towards creating a logo of your own talents and desire, even if you are not professionally competent.

Tool 56: <u>Zillion Designs</u> is an online tool employed not only for logo designing but also for other facilities and tasks which can be made use of by you in case some of them appear appropriate to what your personal platform needs.

Tool 57: <u>Design Hill</u> provides some free tools alongside logo creator, which is why it is advised to take a look and even try these other tools, some of which may be crucial in building your visuals.

Tool 58: <u>Logo Maker</u> with over 10,000 icons, you can explore, build and save unlimited logos in your account for free. You would be requested to purchase your high-resolution logo for it to be downloaded by you.

Tool 59: <u>Logaster</u> is a convenient tool that allows free downloads of small-sized logos to be used by you. You can create variations of your logo and save them all together for future review and comparison.

Tool 60: <u>SquareSpace</u> offers not only the logo maker facility, but also numerous other tools required for starting your own website. Downloading your logo is free unless you need in a high resolution, in the case of which you need to pay 10$.

Tool 61: Logojoy operates through artificial intelligence to design your logo, which is indeed interesting to realize. The engine requires some information from your end about your business, which would assist in creating a logo it finds appropriate to the standards you have mentioned. Registration is required for completing the work and downloading it afterward.

Tool 62: Hipster Logo Generator is about an atmosphere of minimalism, coolness and modernization. It may not be as advanced and complex as other tools but is still the good choice for particular mentalities.

Tool 63: Mark Maker operates simply via typing your business name, followed by generating plenty of available templates from which you can choose for further editing and/or labeling as favorites. The processes of editing and downloading are free of charges.

Tool 64: <u>Vectr</u> is considered more advanced than many other tools yet still does not demand the experience of a designer. It is available in both online and offline forms and is characterized by being quite easy to learn.

Tool 65: <u>Logo Foundry</u> is an application intended for Android and iOS, making logo creating smoother and on the go for millions of enthusiasts and users of these two systems.

Tool 66: <u>Logo Garden</u> includes a spectrum of logo templates from which you can choose by the industry type and other standards of your preference.

Tool 67: <u>Logo Genie</u> operates by simply entering the name of your business, followed by generation of a plenty of templates from which you can pick, edit and settle on.

Tool 68: <u>Logo Yes</u> , despite being simpler and perhaps less intriguing than other tools, is still considered straightforward and preferable to many. It provides hundreds of templates and shapes that are eligible to be included in a logo. Also, editing and downloading your logo are totally free.

Tool 69: <u>LogoPony</u> allows you to take a sneak peak on how your logo would look like on business cards and letterheads. It entails registration so as for you to edit and download the logo.

Tool 70: <u>Logo Master</u> is known to operate through artificial intelligence. You just enter your company name and afterward choose the type of your logo according to your preferences.

Section 5: Free Fonts

Tool 71: Google Fonts is the first line and first choice sought by millions of designers, which is known to appear among the very first results of inputting it in search engines. Google Fonts allow not only utilizing the fonts online, but also downloading them.

Tool 72: Font Squirrel is another font source that can be relied on to acquire plenty of attractive fonts, some of which may be licensed, which entails in turn more caution in the course of finding an appropriate font.

Tool 73: FontSpace, with over 30,000 free fonts contributed by over 2,000 designers, is considered an attractive spot for millions around the world who are fans of downloading and using fonts quite frequently.

Tool 74: <u>DaFont</u> is another popular base for font download. Some fonts are copyright reserved on this platform, which calls for the need to ensure multiple times before going for a particular font.

Tool 75: <u>Abstract Fonts</u> is an online base that includes a curated collection of high-quality fonts. Only some of the fonts are expected to be copyright reserved, calling for the importance of paying attention to focus on the copyright free ones exclusively.

Tool 76: <u>Behance</u> is not defined exactly as a platform for fonts yet more like a social network where designers create portfolios of their best work and share designs they have created with each other.

Tool 77: <u>FontStruct</u> is special for being a font-building tool that allows you an opportunity to create your own fonts with various geometrical shapes. The gallery of the site has so far accommodated more than 43,000 fonts. Most of these fonts are actually created by ordinary people and even non-designers. All these fonts are available to download.

Tool 78: 1001 Fonts includes over 9000 fonts, all available for commercial use without copyright restrictions. Hence the emphasis of not taking the words literally and not misjudging at first sight, is here more intense.

Tool 79: Urban Fonts is another place to find free fonts, which you can search by colors and themes. Creating an account also aids you in saving the fonts of your preference.

Tool 80: FontSpring is a premium marketplace hosting premium font families. It however allows downloading a couple of free fonts from these font families to use with your various projects.

Section 6: Free Graphic Design Tools

Tool 81: Google Drawings is considered by many people a good replacement for the Windows Paint programme that was indeed not that convenient especially for those characterized by accuracy and being minute and to the point when it comes to designing.

Tool 82: HubSpot's 10 Infographic Templates aid you in creating professionally looking infographics with saving hours of time in the process. A good thing is that it is quite easy to customize these templates by the criteria and industry chosen by you.

Tool 83: Canva is a prominent free online platform that helps you to design many visuals such as social media posts, covers, PDF files and presentations.

Tool 84: HubSpot's 50 Customizable CTA Templates are another series of available templates that can be checked through the link and worked on, also with the flexibility of these templates according to the preferences of the designer.

Tool 85: PlaceIt allows you to upload photos directly into enabled stock photo templates. It is expected to eventually enjoy watching the chosen screenshots coming to life.

Tool 86: HubSpot's 5 PowerPoint SlideShare Templates are a good aid of designing presentations, especially for those still experiencing some difficulties regarding utilizing Microsoft PowerPoint and/or the other relevant templates and tools.

Tool 87: Pictaculous is a colorful tool that allows you to take control of a graphic using a palette-like creation tool.

Tool 88: ColorZilla is a great tool that can satisfy your needs that may range from the most basic to your most advanced color-related ones.

Tool 89: <u>Awesome Screenshot</u> can be used as a constant element in your browser, especially when you need to work on multiple screenshots simultaneously.

Tool 90: <u>Snappa</u> is a creative tool employed in marketing. It can be used for various sorts of graphics, including all social media channels. It also has a direct output to Buffer which is in turn a well-known social medium.

Tool 91: <u>BeFunky</u> is an online design tool that can be used not only as a graphic designing tool but also as a photo editor and a collage maker. It also does offer useful tutorials and tips so as for you to be able to create even more fabulous designs and edit your photos with more talent and professionalism.

Tool 92: <u>Skitch</u> is a tool supported by Evernote, oriented to those who are interested in conveying their design through art and visuals, more than those bunches of words that may even be not that influential. Users can use different shapes, arrows, texts, and doodles to annotate their images regardless of their source and its genuineness. They can also file them away to their Evernote accounts for future reference.

Tool 93: Pablo is a simple and easy tool created by Buffer, which is the same website mentioned above. Three main elements construct the entire interface of it: a picture gallery located on the left, a graphic content area located in the middle, plus a customization tab located on the right.

Tool 94: Recite This is a wonderful tool for creating stylish and appealing quote images to be employed for your future social media posts or your future blog. The steps are quite typical: Simply paste the quote into the desired template, which in turn you can alter anytime you want.

Tool 95: Tinkercad aids you to create 3D designs and graphics online. The procedure simply consists of you selecting the shapes you want to use, adjusting them according to your preference and desire to create a design you like. Finally, you can combine the shapes and enjoy the outcome of what you have come up with.

Tool 96: <u>Tiff</u> is created to define which font is more appropriate and belonging as per its "perspective". It allows you to review and compare, and to observe the visual difference and contrast between two fonts by some methods such as layering them on each other. .

Tool 97: <u>CreateBrief</u> will help you with choosing your brief. It is often important to have a "brief" before proceeding any further in the process of creation. You can also use free design brief templates or create your own.

Tool 98: <u>Infogr.am</u> as the name implies, it is employed in creating infographic material, with this material including several media by the involved case.

35

Tool 99: <u>Piktochart</u> allows you creating popular and powerful infographics. Over 600 free templates are available for utilization. The option of creating attractive printables and presentations is also present.

Section 7: Free Video Editing Tools

Tool 100: Magisto is available as an application that is handy by millions of people interested.

Tool 101: Video Toolbox is a free online platform that edits your video and also analyses it to give you highly detailed information about the necessary details of the image. It is also used by many as a video converter tool.

Tool 102: Mixmoov provides a chance to import videos for editing, mainly from YouTube, although the disadvantage comprises the incapability of previewing the finished work before irreversible saving.

Tool 103: Creaza has an interesting set of video editing tools that can be even compatible and convenient for different ages. It can be hence utilized in school projects and thesis submission by high education personalities.

37

Tool 104: <u>Kizoa</u> has a library loaded with lots of animations that can be utilized to customize videos by the specific personal needs of the designer. There is no need for registration to enjoy full services – this can be done without taking that step.

Tool 105: <u>ClipChamp</u> is beneficial when video editing entails conversion and compression, which may not be available in numerous other platforms.

Tool 106: <u>PowToon</u> is a good choice to create videos that are aimed to be explanatory or illustrative.

Tool 107: <u>Online Video Cutter</u> is a web application known to be user-friendly and supplied with advanced editing tools. Users can easily benefit from these tools such as rotating their videos, cropping them, trimming or applying several editing features. This platform is capable of handling a maximum file size of 500MB. Using this platform at all its stages is considered free.

Tool 108: <u>WeVideo</u> is known as a shared online video creation base, which means you can work on a video in partnership with several others. This hence provides an enjoyable environment for collaboration. This platform does also allow another convenient facility which includes saving your work on Google Drive instead of consuming additional space on your computer, sometimes to an unwanted extent.

Tool 109: <u>Wideo</u> is another website for video editing that is considered great by many users, with which you are provided the chance to use the drag and drop feature to create a sequence of animations. You are also given freedom to upload your own images or import from other online platforms not only images but also video footage and audio files.

Section 8: Free Animation and GIF Creating Tools

Creation of animated pictures is believed to render the platform of yours to be created online, more vibrant and appealing to the audience to explore and navigate within. It is even believed to create more beauty than what standard stagnant images do, though it is still highly preferred to have the latter embedded as an indispensable element.

Some online bases that enable you as a non-designer to experience animating your online space are depicted as follows:

Tool 110: MakeAGif.com is one of the most popular GIF creating platforms, on which you are allowed the opportunity to create GIF from pictures, directly from your webcam, from YouTube videos or from a personal video of yours. You are also allowed via this base to upload the GIF you create so as for the website to host it, and for you to be able to share the link of the GIF you have created on other internet media.

Tool 111: <u>Picasion</u> is another prominent platform that is special for the following features:

-You can import media, including photos or videos, from other bases such as Flickr and Picasa.

-It is a multilingual platform, with English, Spanish, Portuguese and Russian being the languages available for users so far.

-You can further edit your images used in the animation, as in adjusting their sizes.

-Its disadvantage nevertheless is that it can sometimes be congested with advertisements.

Tool 112: <u>Meme Center</u> is another well-known platform that allows you to create GIFs from multiple media files, including photos and videos of various sources. You can also further modify your GIF by adding text to it.

41

Tool 113: <u>Giphy</u> is known to be the largest GIF search engine. It has been recently further developed towards making it available for users to not only search for suitable GIFs but also create their own work. This is fulfilled via pasting the URL of the wanted video or dragging and dropping the video into the required field in the creator, in case the wanted video happens to be a computer file.

Tool 114: <u>Imgur</u> is a popular GIF sharing and hosting web bases. It allows the creation of GIFs from pre-existing videos online. This can be fulfilled merely through pasting the URL of the chosen video into the specified field, followed by following the required steps that appear afterward and lead to successfully creating the animation.

Tool 115: <u>Imgflip</u> is another GIF creating a base that is peculiar for enabling you to create your GIF using two variants: either with pictures or with videos. For the former you can upload a collection of images which can be edited to bring out an animated form. As for the latter, you can either upload the video or paste its link, depending on the location of the video needed to be incorporated.

It is quite probable that you would be requested to sign up before proceeding to create your animated work. This platform does also provide a Pro version with which you can upload videos with size exceeding 35 MBs.

Tool 116: EZGif.com is another GIF tool that allows creating of your GIF through uploading a video of your own or pasting the URL of the needed video present online.

Tool 117: Gickr is another free GIF creating base that allows a chance to use several sources, including YouTube, Picasa and your own photo gallery. Its disadvantage may be only the fact that it cannot be utilized while disconnected from the internet.

Tool 118: <u>GIFMaker.me</u> is considered more or less a much simpler tool as it is mainly employed in creating GIFs from a collection of photos. You can upload up to 300 photos, from which altogether a GIF would be created. You can mobilize and drag your photos to position them in a proper order for the GIF to be created.

Tool 119: <u>Gimp</u> is a free online editing tool that allows editing pictures, creating GIFs and creating movie slides. It can be accessed online and is used by so many, despite not being as efficient and advanced as some other resembling programmes. Also, some basic editing features are lacking, which stands for the disadvantage of this online base.

Tool 120: <u>UnFREEz</u>, despite being quite simple and lacking numerous advanced features usually present in almost all the other available tools, it is still deemed an approachable tool, characterized by flexibility and easiness of utilization.

Conclusion

Congratulations! Thank you very much for reading all the way to the end. You've made it through the book and now will be able to save your money and time on creating visuals for web and social networks. Hopefully, you have got some tips and insights from this book that will stick with you forever. Even if it was only one helpful tip, it might create a big difference in your future design projects.

Now I'd like to ask for a "small favour." if you enjoyed this book, would you be kind enough to leave a review for this book on Amazon? It'd be greatly appreciated!

Good Luck and Thank you!

Sage T

www.ingramcontent.com/pod-product-compliance
Lightning Source LLC
Chambersburg PA
CBHW031430250726
48656CB00002B/918